Wheels around Perthshi

by Robert Grieves

One of my own favourite transport scenes is this view of Crianlarich in 1938, captured by the late John Thomas of Springburn, railway historian of renown. It totally encapsulates the era, with the double-headed steam train departing from the nearby station, the archetypal AA patrolman astride his

yellow-liveried B.S.A. motor cycle combination, and Glasgow registered (GE 8250) Singer saloon car of 1930. Detailing further, the Fort William bound L.N.E.R. train heading across the viaduct was hauled by twin "Glen" class 4-4-0 locos headed by 9490 Glen Dessary, built in 1920 at Cowlairs works for the North British Railway and which became 62489 with British Railways until its withdrawal in 1959. Geographically, Crianlarich is a natural junction for road and rail systems, situated where three passes meet. The old Callander & Oban railway arrived from the east through Glen Dochart while the West Highland line came up from the south via Glen Falloch, both continuing via Strathfillan, although on opposite sides of the valley and proceeding to Oban and Fort William respectively. The location has changed little over the years and is still recognisable today at this junction where the A82 road from Glasgow and Loch Lomond to Tyndrum and Fort William meets the A85 for Lochearnhead, Crieff and Perth. The roadside petrol pumps have gone as has the old signpost originally erected by the Scottish Automobile Club and no one, kilted or otherwise, would dare to stand chatting in the road at this busy corner nowadays. Ben More, of course, never changes and continues to tower above the village.

Prior to World War 1 there were few motor passenger services in Perthshire and most journeys were undertaken by rail, with onward connections available at certain stations by horse-drawn coach. One of the first regular motor facilities was provided in 1910 by Cameron of Kinloch Rannoch who owned the local garage and also the village bakery, grocery and ironmonger store. He secured the contract to carry the mails between Pitlochry and Kinloch Rannoch and his earliest motor on this service was this dual-purpose vehicle for mail and passengers, completely built by Argyll Motors of Alexandria.

Acknowledgments

A.K. Bell Library, Perth; British Commercial Vehicle Museum, Leyland; Allan Condie; Alan Cross; Jim Docherty; Ian Maclean; Roy Marshall; The Omnibus Society; John Sinclair.

Introduction

This nineteenth book in the Wheels series contains the usual mix of nostalgic Scottish transport scenes, again with emphasis on road transport. I have regarded Perthshire as it was prior to 1975 when the county boundaries altered after local government re-organisation, in the process losing some areas such as Callander and Crianlarich and gaining others, notably Kinross. This is why certain locations no longer in the Perthshire of today are included. Perth itself does not feature as this was the subject of a previous title, Wheels around Perth and as with the others in the series, this book does not claim to be exhaustive but merely a nostalgic dip into a random range of yesterday's wheels which should hopefully kindle a few memories.

Another early example of a pioneering passenger-carrying vehicle in the area was this Albion open wagonette operated on the Royal Mail contract between Pitlochry and Kirkmichael in 1911 and owned by Charles C. Stuart Ltd., of Pitlochry, well known at that time as the town's local baker, grocer and wine merchant. Although operating the motor mail for five years until the contract ended in 1916, Stuarts were not garage proprietors, these services being provided by Robertson & Gulland, George Watson, J.B. Dean & Son, James Scott & Sons and Marcus Russell's Pitlochry Motor Company. As was the custom in the early years of the automobile, larger hotels in the town including Pitlochry Hydro, Fisher's, Atholl Palace and Scotland's Hotel also provided garaging and repair facilities for their motoring guests.

From Victorian times Perthshire's wonderful scenery was a magnet for the tourist and Aberfeldy was one of several popular centres in the county favoured by visitors. The first proprietors of motorised charabancs to cater for the tourist trade in this area were brothers Alexander and William McKercher, originally from Acharn, where Alex had been the local blacksmith. This scene from 1912 at the 16th century Breadalbane Hotel, Kenmore (now Kenmore Hotel) shows V 1515 and BM 1273, both 20 seat, 25 h.p. solid tyred charabancs built by Commer Cars of Luton. These were used on a service between Aberfeldy Station and Kenmore, carrying mainly railway passengers in connection with the steamer sailings on Loch Tay. Both vehicles had their bodywork raised to the rear, thus providing unobstructed vision over the heads of those in front. The canvas side curtains provided another comfort feature, giving a degree of protection against wind and rain, although obscuring the view at the same time. With no space available elsewhere for luggage, a number of suitcases have been loaded on the roof of the leading charabanc. The advertisement appeared in 1920 and shows one of McKercher's Arrol-Johnston hire cars dating from Edwardian times.

4

Prior to the Great War, Alex. McKercher's garage business was based in Kenmore and then moved to the Crown Hotel garage in Aberfeldy where a Ford agency was obtained. A further move was made to the nearby Breadalbane Hotel garage from where bus services were developed to Killin via both sides of Loch Tay. Also operated was the Lawers mail and passenger service from Aberfeldy to Kenmore and Acharn, back to Kenmore, then Fearnan and Lawers. Other operations ran from Aberfeldy to Kinloch Rannoch plus a further mail contract between Kinloch Rannoch and Rannoch Station. A more ambitious run started in December 1926 linking Kenmore, Aberfeldy, Grandtully, Dalguise, Dunkeld, Birnam, Bankfoot and Perth, which was exchanged with Walter Alexander in the early 1930s for that company's Aberfeldy to Pitlochry service. A range of different makes of bus including A.E.C., Albion, Chevrolet, Cottin et Desgouttes, Ford, Leyland, Minerva and Reo was operated over the years. Illustrated in the late 1940s is GS 3228 of 1932, a blue Bedford fourteen seater seen under the silent gaze of Schiehallion in the village of Kinloch Rannoch. The Rannoch services were relinquished in the 1950s, passing to Donald Steele and later to James Duncan of Kinloch Rannoch while the Aberfeldy Motor Coaches part of the business was sold to Alexander (Midland) in 1974 along with a couple of Willowbrook bodied Bedfords. The remaining garage business in Aberfeldy was bought in 1976 by Stewart's Aberfeldy Motor Services, a company which today continues to operate a high quality coaching business.

Amongst the variety of vehicles in the car hire fleet owned by McKercher of Aberfeldy in the early years was ES 1961, an Overland 18-20 h.p. tourer of 1915. It was finished in dark green and built by the Willys-Overland Co. of Toledo, Ohio. This scene from 1916 shows two fashionably dressed ladies accompanied by a gentleman in military uniform enjoying a chauffeur driven excursion in the Perthshire countryside.

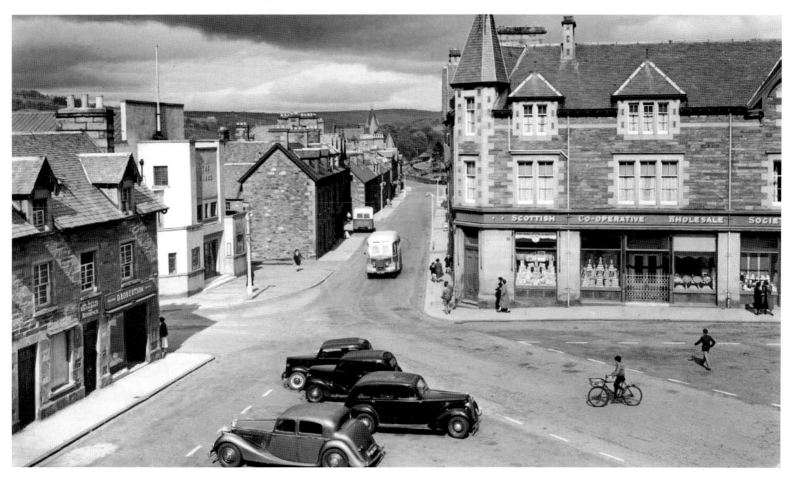

Aberfeldy Square is seen in 1952 with a variety of wheels visible, including a traditional "message bike" being pedalled by a small boy with a few deliveries in the front basket. The nearest of the parked cars is BWS 502, a sleek 1.5 litre 1938 Jaguar, with a Hillman 14, also dating from 1938, alongside. Driving towards the camera along Dunkeld Street and bound for Fearnan is GS 9113, a twenty seater Bedford WTB type bus which had been new to McKercher of Aberfeldy in 1939, passing to Aberfeldy Motor Coaches in 1952 along with the Loch Tayside services. The parked bus is a wartime Bedford OWB type owned by the Aberfeldy branch of the Scottish Co-operative Wholesale Society Ltd. which operated the Aberfeldy-Fortingall-Invervar-Innerwick-Glenlyon run originally served by David Fraser of Aberfeldy. The Co-op. premises survive in business in the square, as does the Birks art deco former cinema building.

Left: When Scotland was still largely in its motoring infancy, the well-to-do members of the Scottish Automobile Club led by its secretary, Robert J. Smith, decided to hold a reliability trial for touring cars in 1905. This proved so successful that further trials were organised for the following few years, all covering a wide area of demanding territory, mainly in the Highlands. Friday 15th June, 1906 was the date of this photograph taken as the competing cars arrived in the late afternoon at Pitlochry, where an overnight stop was made at Fisher's Hotel. Officially numbered 2-40 for the trial and registered G 874 in Glasgow, this was a 16 h.p. Kelvin car, built in small numbers by the Bergius Car & Engine Co. of Glasgow, better known later for the production of Kelvin marine engines. The car was driven by the company's founder and managing director, Walter Bergius, and is seen in the main street watched by a large audience of the Pitlochry populace who very probably had never seen so many motor vehicles together (there were 84 participants). ES 226, the Perthshire registered Renault following the Kelvin was not a competitor in the trial.

Right: The old established Amulree Hotel played host, particularly in Edwardian times, to many affluent motorists or automobilists as they were then generally known who used it as a base before setting out to climb the arduous Amulree hill road, which was then regarded as a daunting drive with gradients up to 1 in 3.5 and ascending over 800 feet in 2 miles. Three cars of that era along with their chauffeurs, owners and passengers pose outside the hotel around 1908. The cars are unable to be identified but are from Bradford and Lincoln respectively, indicating perhaps that a group of motoring friends from England were spending time touring Perthshire.

Left: The Rolls Royce was generally known as "the best car in the world" and recognised everywhere as a symbol of quality. A testing tour over Scottish roads was undertaken in 1909 by Claude Johnson, at that time managing director of Rolls Royce Ltd. at the wheel of Derbyshire registered R 567, a new 6 cylinder 40/50 h.p. model named "Silver Phantom" with Barker touring coachwork. It is seen here in Perthshire negotiating one of a succession of severe hairpin bends above Garrow Farm in Glen Quaich on the isolated Amulree hill road heading towards Kenmore with Loch Freuchie visible in the distance.

Right: The road through the hills which links Blairgowrie in Perthshire with Braemar on Royal Deeside climbs amongst the Grampians to attain a height of 2199' at Cairnwell summit on the Aberdeenshire border, thus giving it the honour of the highest road in Britain. This delightful Edwardian scene near the top shows the motoring apparel typical of the time, when goggles were often worn, in addition to appropriate clothing, to counteract the dust thrown up from the unsealed roads. MS 150, registered in Stirlingshire, was a French-built De Dion Bouton tonneau dating from 1905. The loose surface of the Glenshee road was eventually sealed in 1926 from the county boundary at Cairnwell to the Lair (11 miles) with the next section to Dalrulzion completed the following year.

This was the worst of several fearsome zig-zag bends on the section of the Blairgowrie to Braemar road known as the Devil's Elbow. Improvements over the years have removed the hairpins but also in some respects part of the charm of this scenic road, formerly regarded by many motorists as a bit of an adventure. Very noticeable is the dreadful road surface, unsealed and stony, endured on the Devil's Elbow road prior to re-surfacing after World War 1. The car is a Paisley-built Arrol Johnston 12/15 h.p. tourer of 1908, whose driver is paying scant regard to the number one rule of the road. Admittedly the number of vehicles at that time was very small and therefore the odds against meeting another motorist, especially on this road, were long indeed in those days.

DEVILS ELBOW. MAY 1951.

Left: Winter weather lingered long into 1951 as evidenced in this view taken in May of that year as CGG 888, a Morris Eight series E tourer drives between a double wall of snow at the Devil's Elbow. This particular model dating from 1939 had only a short production run and was not built after the 1939-45 hostilities ended. It would thus be valuable today and even more so because of its treble eight Glasgow registration number.

Right: This view from a Vauxhall in the 1950s shows the warning sign on approach to the Devil's Elbow from the Braemar side, closely followed by another which alerted drivers to the impending double bend. Today there are no such problems on the re-aligned Glenshee road and the one time hazards of the old Devil's Elbow are now but memories.

Drochaid Bhan (the White Bridge) lives up to its name in this snowy scene from the mid 1920s. It lies on the former main A82 road through Strathfillan, between Crianlarich and Tyndrum and is not visible from the present highway. The car on the banks of the River Cononish, a tributary of the Fillan, is GB 6442, a Clyno tourer of 1924. The Clyno was built in Wolverhampton and was one of a very wide range of British-built cars available during the 1920s. This was a particularly popular model at the time and even rivalled the better known Morris Cowley for a period. However, success was relatively short-lived and the company closed in 1930 after only nine years in business.

Road accidents are not a new phenomenon. This collision took place in 1915 on the old north road (which became the A9 after road numbering was introduced) near Birnam at Little Dunkeld where it meets the bridge across the Tay to Dunkeld. The signpost points left to Birnam, Murthly and Perth and right to Aberfeldy while an additional road sign has been erected by the Scottish Automobile Club indicating that Crieff is 22 miles distant and Carlisle 155. The contretemps with the cars was between ES 1806 of 1915, a new model T Ford and SP 1670, a Fife registered Darracq of 1912. The Perthshire vehicle was a locally owned hire car based at the Atholl Arms Hotel in Dunkeld, owned by Thomas Menzies. Mustering around the mishap is the inevitable swarm of spectators, including several in military uniform, but as yet there is no sign of the constabulary.

Left: Cyclecars were very popular small and simple automobiles in the era from shortly before World War 1 until the early 1920s when they virtually disappeared with the advent of cheaper mass-produced cars such as the Austin Seven. This is a typical two seat cyclecar built by Humber of Coventry in 1913, although pictured in 1931 with its owner Allan Hynd of Abernyte. Allan was in his upper eighties at the time and is seen driving home from Perth market on the main Perth-Dundee road near Inchture, then only single carriageway. The car was an air-cooled model, known as the Humberette and some forgotten features of yesteryear include the manually air-activated bulb horn, the acetylene lamps, the handbrake lever outside the bodywork and the empty circular rim which should have held the spare spoked wheel. Registered in Angus with the once familiar SR letters, the car was probably purchased originally from Rossleigh Motors, the Humber dealer in Dundee at the time.

Right: The tree-lined avenue which was the Muthill road outside Crieff at the time of this view from 1914 has not altered to any degree. TS 985 was a 7 h.p. Swift cyclecar purchased new that year by James Bain White of Dundee, well known for his picture postcard business; it was not unknown for him to include his own car in his compositions in order to enliven an otherwise quiet scene. The Swift Company of Coventry had originally built sewing machines and bicycles before progressing to cars and although achieving a fair degree of success, could not compete with the big boys of the motor industry and ceased business in 1931.

The natural beauty of Perthshire has for long been a tourist magnet and no area more so than the Trossachs, helped in popularity in the 19th century by the writings of Sir Walter Scott. The illustration shows the recognised mode of travel from the Trossachs Hotel at the dawn of the 20th century, before motor vehicles slowly but surely started their dominance over horse-drawn transport. Two well-to-do ladies set out for a carriage drive in the capable hands of their immaculately uniformed coachman on the box seat in front. Although such a conveyance was often drawn by a single horse, on this occasion it is pulled by a matching pair. Open carriages such as this were often referred to as "sociables" and the folding hood could of course be raised for protection on any of the rainy days which just might be experienced in the Trossachs.

On a winter's day looking north in the village of Strathyre in the late 1920s. The street is almost deserted apart from a distant parked car and another in the foreground, with its radiator muffled against the cold as it stands outside the Strathyre Inn on the now busy A84 road between Callander and Lochearnhead. This was SC 2123, one of the very earliest examples of a Morris Minor and was registered in Edinburgh in November 1928. The original Minor was introduced that year to compete with the very successful baby Austin Seven which was similar in appearance. This first edition Minor, however, did not achieve the same degree of popularity and ceased to be built in 1934. The name was of course revived when the car was re-introduced at the first post-war motor show at London's Earls Court in 1948 and the second generation Minor and later Morris 1000 continued with a remarkably successful production run until the early 1970s. A non-motoring but nonetheless interesting feature of this photograph is the early cigarette vending machine against the wall of the inn.

This cottage was the last thatched house in the Trossachs area of Perthshire and continues to be a family home today, albeit no longer thatched and considerably changed in appearance. The bulk of Sron Armailte (peak of the army) broods over the tranquil scene with smoke from the village chimneys drifting slowly in the air on a still summer day in 1926. The only sound to disturb the rural peace would be the approach of ES 8752 which was a new Standard tourer, registered in the county with those once-familiar letters. When the ES numbers reached 9999 in January 1928, GS was introduced as the next motor registration index lettering system for Perthshire. Researching some of the earlier motor vehicles in the county, the same picture emerged as elsewhere in Scotland in that it was only the wealthier members of the community who had the means to make a wheeled purchase, particularly prior to the Great War. Accordingly the motor register of that time shows such names as Patrick Ness of Braco Castle, Albert Pullar of Perth, Alexander Blair of the Bailie Nicol Jarvie Hotel, Aberfoyle, Arthur Bell of Barclayhills, Douglas Sandeman of Stanley, The Marquis of Tullibardine, Dunkeld House, and Sir Robert Moncreiffe of Moncreiffe, Bridge of Earn to name but a few. By the mid 1920s and the era of the Standard seen above, private motoring was slowly becoming a possibility for many rather than a privilege for the few. The Standard Motor Co. of Coventry built cars over a 60 year span from 1903 until 1963 by which time the company was owned by Leyland Motors. The final model produced was the Vanguard.

Murray Lornie Thomas of Alyth started in the haulage industry in a small way in the early 1920s transporting potatoes to Dundee. Commencing with a model 501 A.E.C. on solid tyres, M.L. Thomas remained faithful to this breed throughout the lifetime of his business and so the Southall-built chassis were a familiar sight in the former weaving town. The fleet jumped in size when in the late 1920s a lucrative contract was won in connection with carrying road materials for the reconstruction of the A9 Perth-Inverness highway. Incredible though it may seem today, right up until the time of these improvements, this vital road was described in parts as "breaking up in dry weather to become gravelly and loose." Another important contract followed in 1929 although somewhat further afield when Thomas obtained the work involved in removing the tram rails uplifted after the closure of the Greenock and Port Glasgow Tramways system. The bulk of the firm's work, however, continued to concentrate on agricultural produce, Alyth being situated in Strathmore, one of Scotland's finest farming areas. Accordingly fleet improvements in the early 1930s comprised the purchase of several A.E.C. Mammoths and Mammoth Majors including Thomas's first diesel-powered lorry in 1932. Also new in 1932 was GS 3004, a six-wheel Mammoth Major seen loading on a gloomy Glasgow day at the docks. The M.L. Thomas business, like so many other transport concerns, succumbed to nationalisation in 1949 and the blue-liveried fleet was painted into the corporate red of British Road Services who maintained the former depot in Alyth for a period before transferring to a new base at Meigle.

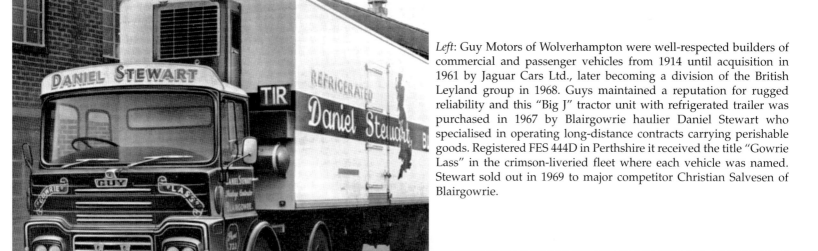

Left: Guy Motors of Wolverhampton were well-respected builders of commercial and passenger vehicles from 1914 until acquisition in 1961 by Jaguar Cars Ltd., later becoming a division of the British Leyland group in 1968. Guys maintained a reputation for rugged reliability and this "Big J" tractor unit with refrigerated trailer was purchased in 1967 by Blairgowrie haulier Daniel Stewart who specialised in operating long-distance contracts carrying perishable goods. Registered FES 444D in Perthshire it received the title "Gowrie Lass" in the crimson-liveried fleet where each vehicle was named. Stewart sold out in 1969 to major competitor Christian Salvesen of Blairgowrie.

Right: Also seen in Blairgowrie, climbing towards the High Street at the Royal Hotel corner, is an earlier vehicle from the same Wolverhampton stable. This was 7536 VX, an Essex-registered Guy Warrior of 1960 hauling a maximum payload of frozen food for its owners, the Smedley food group who operated a cannery in Haugh Road, Rattray. Along with other lorries it performed a regular 1000 mile return journey from the fertile fields of Angus and Perthshire, where Smedleys owned a number of farms providing the produce for their canned fruit and vegetables, to a variety of drops at destinations in the south of England.

Left: Perhaps Perthshire's leading transport operator of the 1920s was Peter Crerar of Crieff who not only ran a large fleet of charabancs for touring but also constructed their bodywork in his own coachworks in the town. Additionally, bus services were operated over an area between Callander, Crieff and Perth while Perth city services were run in partnership with Hepburn of Perth under the fleet name Perth General Omnibus Company in direct competition with the local municipal public transport provided by Perth Corporation. Peter Crerar was a true entrepreneur, also owning cinemas and hotels in addition to his thriving transport business. This view shows some of his charabancs on tour in 1926 led by an Italian Lancia and followed by six French-built Cottins et Desgouttes, all with Crerar's own bodywork. The location is the junction known as the Fiveways at Dunblane, where the old signpost pre-dated road numbering and stood in the middle of what became the A9 highway. It is pointing to Bridge of Allan, Stirling and Sheriffmuir, with the arm to Auchterarder and Perth not totally visible. Dunblane Hydro Hotel is in the background.

Right: Peter Crerar's many and varied businesses included the operation of pleasure sailings on Loch Earn from St. Fillans to Lochearnhead in clever conjunction with his own charabancs bringing customers from a wide area around. Here we see Peter's twin-screw steamer Queen of Loch Earn coming through the streets of Crieff hauled by a horse-drawn wagon after sailing to Perth on delivery from the boatbuilders Forbes Bros. of Rosehearty in 1922. When Crerar sold his transport interests to the powerful Scottish General Omnibus Company in 1928 the deal included this vessel and in 1932 when the S.G.O.C. was acquired on behalf of the S.M.T. group of companies by Alexanders it then passed to control of the Falkirk firm. Alexanders continued to operate coach tours in connection with the sailings on Loch Earn until the pleasure boat was withdrawn in 1936 and converted for use as a houseboat, moored near St. Fillans. Interestingly this was not Alexander's final nautical link as in 1969 the Loch Lomond steamer Maid of the Loch came under their control when ownership passed from the Caledonian Steam Packet Co. to the Scottish Transport Group and remained so until withdrawal of the Maid in 1981.

The train from Glasgow has delivered buoyant business to the charabancs of the Trossachs Hotel Company, seen here fully loaded outside Callander Railway Station in 1926. They are ready to depart for Kilmahog, Loch Vennachar, The Trossachs and Loch Katrine where the happy horde will transfer to the steamer Sir Walter Scott for a cruise on the famous waters (the grand old vessel continues to sail there to this day). The charabanc fleet at that time was of Albion and Lancia manufacture and this view shows, from the left, six Albion 14 seaters dating from 1920 including ES 2970 and 3182 then three Lancia 18 seaters (ES 4785, 4786 of 1922 and 7432 of 1925) while on the extreme right is the latest addition to the fleet, an 18 seat Albion "Viking" of 1926 (ES 8504). All these charabancs conformed to the restrictive 6' width limit which then applied to vehicles using the Trossachs roads. Certain sections of the road are no wider today, yet no such restrictions apply to the huge tri-axle coaches which squeeze along "where twines the path", to quote from Sir Walter Scott's "Lady of the Lake", a novel which contributed so much to boost tourism in this area..

John Imrie Great and William John Adam of Alyth operated the rural Glenisla mailbus service between Alyth, Dykends, Glenisla and Folda for over half a century from the mid 1920s. It had been pioneered in the days of horse-drawn coaches by Valentine of Alyth, later passing to Ewart of Alyth. Small Ford Chevrolet and Fiat buses were used in the early years and a number of cars and taxis were also owned for private hire purposes. One of these was VA 528, a second-hand but nonetheless imposing Daimler landaulette dating from 1922 which featured a folding hood over the rearmost section, making this a semi-open car when required. Apart from carrying letters, parcels and passengers, the mailbus often carried more unusual items including rabbits, which proliferated in Glenisla and would be sold to butchers and game dealers in the surrounding villages.

Left: Winter weather often plies Perthshire with severe snowfalls, playing havoc with road conditions and public transport. In the particularly wicked winter of 1947 Ed Robb, one of the local postmen based at Alyth, had to strap on skis in order to complete his deliveries in the Mains of Glenisla area. In the background can be seen GS 2351, the Glenisla mailbus owned for over 20 years by Great and Adam of Alyth. This Ford was fitted with chains around its tyres for a large part of the snow season to provide traction for its daily duties during the worst of the weather.

Right: On Saturday nights Great & Adam operated buses from Alyth to Newtyle, Coupar Angus and Blairgowrie in connection with late dances although the Glenisla mail was their main service and the view above shows the regular mailbus for many years. This was GS 2351, a neat wee Ford 7-seater with space for goods, parcels and post in the rear of the saloon. Purchased new in 1931, it was still in service with the company in the mid 1950s and is seen at Folda (where the mail was sorted in a small hut) with its usual driver, long-serving employee John Stronach, who was later awarded the British Empire Medal for service to the public. Many years ago John recalled to me that on Saturdays the bus made a double run up Glenisla and it was common for many of the glen folk to cycle down to Alyth from where they would travel by train to Dundee, returning to catch the evening bus back home, which would have as many as a dozen bicycles perched on the roof on the uphill journey.

The main road north from Blairgowrie divides at Bridge of Cally in Strath Ardle, the left fork leading to Kirkmichael and Pitlochry and the right to Glenshee and Braemar. The former petrol pumps at Bridge of Cally Hotel would therefore be in regular demand, offering a choice of fuel in this mid 1930s scene between Pratts and Mex at 1/4d per gallon. Being filled by the attendant is GS 1687 a 1930 B.S.A. motorcycle which has opted for Pratt's petrol. Parked outside the hotel is GS 843, a 1929 Ford model A "Fordor" (with four doors, as opposed to the "Tudor" two door model) while to the right is an Austin Ten saloon of around 1934.

Although now in Clackmannanshire, Pool of Muckhart was formerly a Perthshire village lying in the lee of the Ochil Hills on the A 91 road between Dollar and Kinross. This delightful scene dates from the summer of 1939. The car is FXE 202, a new Hillman Minx registered in London, whose occupants are presumably on a Scottish touring holiday and enjoying the good weather with the sunshine roof open; note also the Minx's forward opening front door. The driver is smoking so perhaps a brief halt has been made to buy ten Capstan from the dispenser or from Rollo's wee shop at the Ochil Tea Rooms. Possibly the purchase of petrol was the reason for stopping where there was a choice between Shell or Redline at 1/5d per gallon from the kerbside bowsers. According to the sign the tea rooms also offered bed and breakfast with car accommodation and so this was a further option for the tourists. Today this building, largely unchanged, is Mona's of Muckhart coffee shop but the fuel pumps, as in many other rural locations, have gone.

Ancaster Square was the central point in Callander formerly used as a stance for coach tours to the Trossachs and elsewhere. This scene from 1924 shows ES 6568, a new 19 seat Lancia Tetraiota charabanc loading for departure and owned by the Black family of the town's Dreadnought Garage. At that time the dark red liveried fleet also included Fiat, G.M.C., Halley, Reo and Thornycroft makes while in the 1930s Bedfords and Commers featured. The business had started originally with horse-drawn coaches, based at the Dreadnought Hotel stables in the popular tourist town and survived until 1946 when Blacks sold to Dawson & Gordon of Callander. Only one year later this firm was purchased by Walter Alexander of Falkirk along with ten assorted and mainly elderly vehicles, most of which soon went for disposal. Other former coach operators in the area included John Waugh of Callander, the Trossachs Hotel Co., and David Mitchell. Inset is an advert for Waugh's charabanc tours from the early 1920s.

A scene from the late 1950s, again in Callander's Ancaster Square, which at this time was still a departure point for bus services and coach tours from the town. Three very different members of Walter Alexander's "Bluebird" fleet are visible on their respective duties. In the foreground is the oldest, WG 7258, a 1938 Leyland Cheetah bodied by Burlingham of Blackpool (fleet number K 26) and working the Trossachs Pier service in conjunction with Loch Katrine sailings. Alongside is BWG 540 (W 236) a Duple bodied Bedford OB type coach of 1949 and normally used on tour duties. The youngest of the trio is a 1955 Alexander bodied A.E.C. Monocoach numbered in the AC series and which would have been operating the Callander-Stirling-Edinburgh service and based at the Stirling depot. The other two were based at the company's small depot in Callander Main Street which was coded C2. This was Burnside Garage which had been acquired in 1946 with the business of haulage contractor and coach operator David Mitchell who ran green and cream liveried coaches with the fleetname "Cream Line." Mitchell also had cattle floats which were retained by him after sale of the passenger vehicles, none of which were kept by Alexander. Inset is a typical handbill which was usualy affixed to bus windows advising passengers of timetable alterations.

The railway arriving in Callander in 1858 quickly led to the previously quiet village becoming a fashionable Victorian spa resort. This view from Edwardian times shows the station with the morning train from Oban which would carry on to Glasgow via Dunblane and Stirling, the coaches coupled next to the engine continuing through to London Euston. The locomotive was Caledonian Railway 4-6-0 no.54 which was built in 1905 at their St.Rollox Works in Glasgow. On "grouping" of the railway companies in 1923 it became 14608 with L.M.S. and remained in service until 1935. Sadly the scenic Callander and Oban railway line which included the glories and gradients of Glen Ogle was one of the many casualties of the so-called Beeching era and was scheduled to close in November 1965. In fact, a landslide at Glenoglehead caused a premature permanent closure in September that year but today sections of the former line can be walked or cycled as part of the Rob Roy Way.

From Callander, the next station on the Oban line towards Crianlarich was Strathyre where once more we see Caley locomotive no.54. This animated moment from a century ago completely captures the atmosphere of a country railway station of that era. The moustached (weren't they all in those days?) stationmaster looks on as a porter holds up the circular tablet to be exchanged with the engine driver to allow access to the single track section ahead. Further wheels in this view belong to the local carrier's horse-drawn cart for delivering and collecting luggage. Also noteworthy is the ornate heron fountain on a base of Ben Cruachan granite which had been won for the superb station garden in late Victorian times in an early "best kept station" award and fortunately survived closure of the line in 1965. It may now be found in a garden in Strathyre village and not, as some rail enthusiasts believe, in neighbouring Argyllshire on the Oban-bound platform of Dalmally station, which admittedly boasts an identical fountain.

A diesel railbus built by Wickham of Ware passes through Methven Junction in 1961 on a special working over the Crieff-Perth tracks which had been closed to passenger traffic since 1951, although remaining open to freight trains. Back in 1927 the L.M.S. Railway had operated Sentinel steam-powered railcars on the Perth-Methven line. The more modern type illustrated was typical of the small four-wheel single carriage vehicles used as an economy measure after withdrawal of steam operation on several parts of the railway system which could not justify larger trains. However, their unreliable performance meant temporary steam replacement on many occasions. The first line in Scotland to introduce this type of railbus was the branch from Gleneagles in September 1958 serving Tullibardine, Muthill, Strageach Halt, Highlandman, Pittenzie Halt, Crieff and Comrie, although only three daily trains continued to Comrie, all others terminating at Crieff. The year 1964 saw final operations on this 15 mile branch line, when substitute bus services were introduced by Alexander, from their depot in Crieff, where the railbuses had been stabled at the town's small railshed and manned by local crews.

David Fraser pioneered the motor mail service to Fortingall, Bridge of Balgie and Glen Lyon prior to World War 1 from his base in Aberfeldy. His earliest recorded motor vehicle was ES 670, a 16 h.p. Albion wagonette which was purchased new for the mail contract in 1910 and painted blue and red. Jumping onwards by three decades the business was transferred to D.A. Leslie of Aberfeldy but still traded under Fraser's name. The Glen Lyon mail continued to operate during the restrictions of the Second World War when this rural route was maintained with SX 3030, a fourth-hand Thornycroft A2 type which had started life in 1930 working for Rendall's Blue Bus Service of Broxburn, a firm acquired by S.M.T. of Edinburgh in 1932 along with this bus. After only a couple of years it was bought by Cunningham of Paisley who later sold it to Fraser, where it became one of four Thornys in his fleet, three of which had seen former service with S.M.T. and one of which was converted to a lorry for the local haulage side of his business. In this scene at Aberfeldy Station in March 1943, the Thorny has a distinctly weary appearance, evidenced by a cracked front headlamp and a completely bald front nearside tyre, along with wire mesh replacing the glass in some of the windows. Also noteworthy is the single masked headlamp and the mudguard surrounds painted white to comply with wartime regulations. However, it should be remembered that operational difficulties were extreme during this period of the hostilities, with great problems in maintaining high standards, caused by shortages of most items. Despite its less than pristine condition, the folk of Glen Lyon were undoubtedly grateful for their daily transport to town with the elderly omnibus.

Albions in Alyth. A brace of buses await departure in the town square around 1930 when the route between Dundee and Blairgowrie was operated by the green liveried S.M.T. company of Edinburgh which had expanded from their Lothian territory in 1920 by introducing services based in Dundee. On the left is RS 8305 bodied by Cowieson of Glasgow, one of the earliest of the popular 'model 28' type Albions of 1926 which had a long production run until 1932. The Aberdeen registration is explained by this bus having served originaly with Major Sibley's 'Gordon line' service linking Aberdeen and Culter. Alongside is SC 570 which was new to S.M.T. in 1928 with full fronted bodywork by Croall of Edinburgh. Neither bus lasted more than a few years with S.M.T. and both later ran in Walter Alexander's fleet. Close inspection of the front nearside of these buses reveals the small oval licence plates (respectively 79 & 82) which were issued by the authorities in Dundee to passenger vehicles operating through the city. In 1949 routes serving the Dundee, Alyth and Blairgowrie area were amongst those which passed from S.M.T. to Alexander control.

In the 1890s, before motor vehicles came to the county, John Harper started business as a blacksmith and cycle agent in Perth Street, Blairgowrie but as the age of the automobile dawned he was quick to adapt to the new mode of transport and accordingly developed a garage business. By 1919 John Harper & Sons had secured post office contracts for provision of motor mail services between Blairgowrie and Glenshee via Bridge of Cally and Blair to Enochdhu via Bridge of Cally, Ballintuim and Kirkmichael. The vehicles used to operate these services had room to carry a small number of passengers in addition to the mail. This scene outside Blairgowrie Post Office in the mid 1930s shows the two Ford model AA buses which Harper had bought in 1929 to replace earlier Fords on the mail runs. GS 1408 to the left has a laundry hamper loaded on the roof rack, no doubt for delivery to one of the hotels along its regular route to Glenshee. This bus had bodywork by Alexander Motors, the Edinburgh Ford agent, while the Strath Ardle mailbus GS 1388 alongside was bodied by Cadogan of Perth. Both were painted in Royal Mail red livery and while ostensibly fourteen seaters, were converted to seating for eight, in order to accommodate a compartment for mail and parcels.

Heavy snowfalls often provided problems for the transport operators in years gone by when the roads were neither gritted nor cleared by snowploughs, typified by this scene somewhere in Strath Ardle in the early 1930s showing Harper's Ford mailbus GS 1388 experiencing difficulties in the drifts. Around that period there were no less than three firms providing passenger connections between Kirkmichael and Blairgowrie. Apart from Harper, Arthur Melville of Aldchlappie Hotel, Kirkmichael (now the Strathardle Inn) and Tom Reid of Kirkmichael both served Strath Ardle and additionally Hugh McLachlan's service from Bridge of Cally gave further coverage on the section between Cally and Blair. Those were the days when the local folk rarely had their own means of travel and were accordingly much more dependent on public transport.

When the Ford buses seen on p.33 & 34 reached the end of their working lives, John Harper replaced them unusually with two Rolls Royce limousines dating from the 1920s which were suitably rebodied with space for mails, parcels and passengers by coachbuilders McMurray & Archibald of Perth. Both were re-registered with new Perthshire numbers, the first being GS 9739 in 1940 for the mail run from Blairgowrie to Glenshee, followed by GS 9881 in 1941 for the Strath Ardle mail from Blairgowrie to Kirkmichael and Enochdhu. The latter bus is seen in the late 1940s with its regular driver Willie Slidders on what must have been a busier than normal occasion since the Rolls is towing a small trailer.

Left: After the death of John Harper in 1948 his garage and engineering business was bought by J.L. Fraser, managing director of Frew's garage of Perth, who continued the mailbus services under the Harper name but quickly replaced the elderly Rolls Royce buses. Their successors arrived in 1949 and were these two Austin K types (CGS 621/622) which had their standard van bodies converted for mail and passenger purposes by McMurray & Archibald of Perth and both were finished in traditional post office red livery for the mail contracts.

Right: The next stage in the story of the buses from Blairgowrie to Strath Ardle and Glenshee took place in the 1960s by which time the Kirkmichael service had passed in succession from John Harper to Arthur Melville and then to William Keiro, both of Kirkmichael, prior to ownership moving to the Blairgowrie section of A. & C. McLennan of Spittalfield. The Glenshee run also passed in 1964 to McLennan, who continued expansion in 1967 with the acquisition of the long-established service provided by Hugh McLachlan, Bridge of Cally, between Blair, Cally and Blacklunans. Pictured while loading at the former post office in Blairgowrie High Street is RGS 836, a Fordson Thames van new in 1962 to Harper of Blair and specially adapted to operate the mailbus service to Spittal of Glenshee and seen later that decade when working for McLennan. Laundry hampers (see p.33) were still a regular item amongst the variety of goods carried. Today Stagecoach operates the Strath Ardle service which continues beyond Enochdhu to Straloch and Tarvie whereas Glenshee is now served by a Royal Mail postbus.

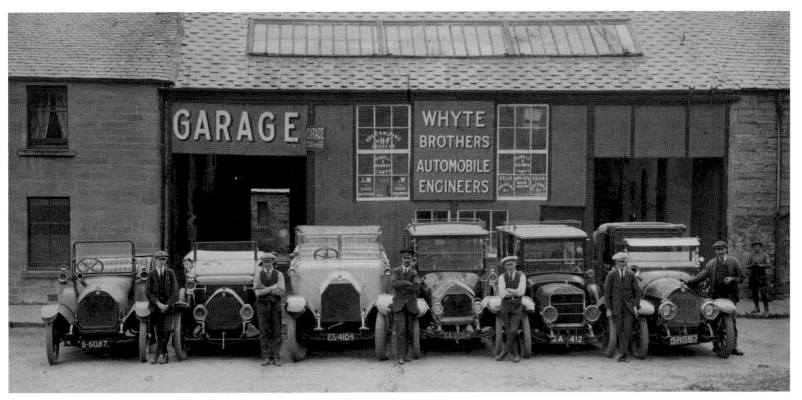

Strathmore Garage in the Wellmeadow, Blairgowrie, photographed shortly after Alf and David Whyte and Dick Farquharson purchased the premises in 1922, was partly financed by their gratuities received after service in the Great War. A previous owner was cycle dealer and motor engineer Rudolph Raitt when the building was known as the Strathmore Cycle Works. The Whytes expanded their garage business to include car hiring and also the provision of local bus services to Bridge of Cally, to Dunkeld via Marlee, Clunie and Butterstone and to Perth, which were sold to the Dundee branch of the giant Scottish Motor Traction Company partly in 1928 and partly in 1939 along with two small Dodge and Chevrolet buses. This row of vehicles owned by Whyte Bros. in the early 1920s shows assorted hire cars and taxis and also what is thought to have been their first charabanc. From the left: Overland S 5087 with Neil Whitton, a Humber (whose number has faded) with Dave Whyte, Lancia charabanc ES 4104 (named Fair Helen) with George Dove, Belsize SA 1294 with Jock Whyte, Singer SA 1412 with Alf Whyte and Benz cabriolet SR 567 with Jim Crawford. Also visible on the extreme right is local boy Will Ewing. In September 1926 an advert appeared in the Perthshire Advertiser announcing the start of Whyte's pioneering link by bus between Blairgowrie and Perth which described their vehicles thus: "They are roomy with double springs to eliminate jolting, therefore ensuring comfort". One of the buses in question was ES 8884, a new 26 seat Minerva built in Belgium while the other was ES 8558, a French built Cottin et Desgouttes, with a charabanc body by Crerar of Crieff.

The brown Bedford buses of the Bankfoot Motor Company were a familiar sight until the early 1960s on the run between Perth, Luncarty, Bankfoot and Waterloo. Alexander Stanley Whyte and James Taylor Whyte had taken over the business from Nicoll of Bankfoot in 1925 and in the pre-war years a variety of different buses worked the route including a few forgotten makes such as A.J.S. Pilot, B.A.T. Cruiser, Berliet, Chevrolet, G.M.C. and Reo. From wartime onwards, Bedfords were the mainstay of the fleet, starting with the infamous wooden-seated utility type of the wartime years. Pictured in 1960 setting out from Kinnoull Street in Perth on its journey to Bankfoot is CGS 766 which was a Bedford OB model new in 1949 with bodywork by Mulliner of Northampton, a builder perhaps better known for high quality coachwork on limousines. In 1961, Bankfoot Motors sold out to Walter Alexander of Falkirk but none of the ageing bus fleet was operated by the new owner.

A well-known name in transport circles for decades was Alexander (Sandy) McLennan who began business on his own account in 1945 when he acquired the existing Spittalfield & District Bus Service owned by Wm. Armstrong of Spittalfield where he had been chief engineer. Armstrong had operated to a variety of surrounding towns and villages including Blairgowrie, Dunkeld, Murthly, Stanley and of course Perth. Further expansion followed in 1946 when McLennan took over the grey and red buses of John Allan & Thos. Scott based in Stanley, providing further routes between Perth and Stanley and from Perth to Errol. Going back to the days of Armstrong's operations, the illustration shows GS 2157, a Leyland Badger of 1930 in the firm's blue livery and seen prior to departure for Spittalfield at the stance in Blairgowrie. The bus behind on the Dunkeld service was Thornycroft GS 2094, also owned by Armstrong, and both vehicles carried bodywork built in Perth by Cadogan's St. Catherine's Road coachworks. The Badger was nominally a goods chassis but could be classified as a normal control (bonneted) version of the Leyland Lion passenger model. Although Leyland received healthy export orders for Badger passenger vehicles (it had good ground clearance), Armstrong's bus was one of few of this model in Britain. Nonetheless it had a long life and continued in service into the 1950s, albeit rebuilt on aquisition by A.& C. McLennan.

A. & C. McLennan improved and extended the services acquired in the early years of the business and also purchased double deck vehicles such as this to cope with increased post-war patronage at a time when few folk could afford their own car. Passenger numbers peaked at this period and remained healthy during the next decade. Witness the long queue boarding at the Kinnoul Street terminus in Perth for the rural run home to Kinclaven after Saturday shopping. This community has now lost its bus link. The bus was ACS 858, a Leyland Titan TD7 bodied by Northern Counties of Wigan which had been new during wartime to Western S.M.T. in 1942 and which ran with McLennan until 1963 albeit with the addition of doors fitted to the open rear platform. This was an improvement carried out at the company's own coachbuilding department in Perth to all the deckers in the fleet in order to provide a little extra passenger comfort.

This scene from the late 1950s shows The Square in Errol with its Victorian jubilee fountain surmounted by a unicorn. The attractive village lies on the north bank of the Firth of Tay in the fertile Carse of Gowrie and half way between Perth and Dundee. About to depart for Perth is JXN 370, one of several former London Transport Park Royal bodied Leyland RTL type buses of 1949 purchased by A. & C. McLennan. Heading in the Dundee direction is one of the older double-deckers which were replaced with the introduction of the RTLs. This was EOG 248, one of six Metro-Cammell bodied Leyland Titan TD6 models of 1939 originally owned by Birmingham Corporation and which came to Perthshire in 1951. This view clearly shows the re-built rear of the bus incorporating the platform doors fitted by McLennan to his double deck fleet which despite being second hand was always maintained in first class condition. Errol had been the home of McIntosh's bus service which plied back and forward the short distance between the village and the station and which was acquired by the expanding McLennan company, which operated the Dundee route from a small sub-depot in the village.

Sandy McLennan, in addition to the bus services, had his finger in many pies including retail stores, a commercial coachbuilding and repair depot, car and commercial vehicle dealerships and agricultural business; there was also a marine department at Perth Harbour responsible for boat building, repairs and chandlery. Sandy even flew his own private plane based at Scone when called further afield to supervise his growing organisation. A further successful branch of the McLennan empire was the development of car delivery transporters at a time when car numbers were increasing rapidly on our roads. This pioneering part of the business started in 1952 with initial distributive connections forged with the Rootes Group although other car builders and dealers also used McLennan's transporters which thus carried a wide range of makes. These transporters were of B.M.C., Commer and Leyland manufacture but in the 1960s McLennan began constructing his own which were built on second hand Leyland Royal Tiger underfloor engined bus chassis. These were stripped down at the Spittalfield workshops then re-conditioned and fitted with lifting and carrying equipment and a single width driving cab where the mate sat behind the driver. They ran from a variety of collection centres in England to distribution points all over Scotland, the longest run being from Southampton Docks to Thurso with continental cars. At the peak of business there were 27 transporters in the fleet and seen above is Leyland GES 438E, converted and re-registered in 1967 from a former Royal Tiger bus. Sandy McLennan died in 1972 but the firm continued under the able management of his former secretary, Margaret Woodman. The car transporter section was sold to Toleman of Linwood followed by the bus business which was bought in 1985 by the then infant Stagecoach company of Perth.

Boss of the business, Sandy McLennan, founder of the firm and a true Scottish entrepreneur, seen at Spittalfield in the 1960s with a variety of his beloved buses. The two 'deckers were Leyland Titan PD1 XG 8202 which started life in 1946 with Middlesbrough Corporation and CRD 253, an AEC Regent which first ran with Reading Corporation in 1947. Sandy stands alongside Leyland Tiger PS1 DGS 536 of 1951, fitted with bodywork equipped for one man operation and constructed in McLennan's own coachbuilding department at Spittalfield, an example of many bodies built in-house by the company.

In the days when the Stagecoach was seen only in western movies, the best known name in buses throughout Perthshire was Alexander. Walter Alexander had originally worked in an iron foundry prior to opening a cycle repair shop in Main Street, Camelon, Falkirk. The rear of this building backed towards Brown Street which was to become a familiar name on the side of the famous fleet of blue buses which were initially garaged at this address where their first charabanc was stabled in 1914. From the early 1920s onwards there was fairly rapid expansion, with new services introduced on a regular basis and a second depot built at Kilsyth. A profitable service between Glasgow and Stirling was continued into Perthshire via Dunblane and Auchterarder to Perth in December 1926, initially with ten buses each way, competing with and hurting the railway company in particular, whose fares were undercut by a considerable margin. Illustrated (minus its spare wheel) is MS 6440, an Albion PK 26 model with bodywork by Northern Counties of Wigan which was no.63 when new in 1926 and one of many similar Albions in the fleet. Its blue paintwork carries what was then the new style Alexander fleet name which became increasingly well-known through the years. It was one of the first buses to operate the extended route from Glasgow into Perthshire although this scene at the city stance in Cathedral Street shows Dundee on a paper destination bill on the front windscreen indicating that the date was sometime after late 1927 by which time the service had been further extended through to the jute city. More progression in 1928 saw Alexander's buses reaching Aberdeen.

Eleven Leyland Tigers await the arrival of a train at Gleneagles Station bringing a large group to a conference at the nearby Gleneagles Hotel in 1929. 33 of these TS1 models had been new to the Alexander fleet that year and fitted with coachwork built by the operator at their Stirling factory. A feature of these 32-seaters was the fitment of a large fold-back canvas roof section which was really only a step away from the days of the open charabanc and only marginally less draughty. Close inspection of the original photo reveals that the routeboards along the luggage hoppers were signwritten for the Glasgow-Perth-Dundee-Montrose-Stonehaven-Aberdeen service which had commenced the previous year but as may be seen, these buses were equally at home on private hire and touring work. Leading the line is MS 8836 which was originally no.153 in the fleet, becoming 453 in 1930 and P61 in a further re-numbering exercise in 1932. In 1935 it was re-bodied by Alexander along with many others of this class, but no longer incorporating the "all-weather" style of roof. The drivers are all wearing Alexander's "touring" uniform of the period incorporating white topped caps, white linen coats with blue collars and cuffs, plus boots and leather gaiters.

Some of the services inherited by Alexander on acquisition of the Scottish General Omnibus Co. of Larbert in 1932 included journeys into Perthshire. These were mainly routes pioneered by Crerar of Crieff such as Crieff-Methven-Perth and Crieff Muthill-Gleneagles-Auchterarder-Dunning-Forteviot-Bridge of Earn-Perth which passed to S.G.O.C. in 1928 when Crerar sold out. The "General", as the company was usually known, also reached into the county with their service from Stirling via Bridge of Allan to Dunblane, which was then part of Perthshire. Alexander extended this service to operate from the mining village of Cowie, through Bannockburn to Stirling and thence to Dunblane. Above we see Alexander's Albion D99 (CP 6240) passing through Bridge of Allan in the mid 1930s en route to the Cathedral City. This was one of many second hand petrol powered buses purchased in that decade (mainly through Glasgow dealers Millburn Motors) which had started their lives in various parts of the British Isles, including Wales and Ireland. D99 had originated with Hebble Motor Services of Halifax in 1927 but was converted to diesel power and rebodied by Alexander before entering their service in 1934.

Perthshire's main traffic artery is the A9 highway which at its northern end passes through Glen Garry into Invernessshire. At the county boundary both road and rail share the desolate Drumochter Pass, through which General Wade built the original military road in 1729 and which a century later was re-aligned by Thomas Telford. The well-known lines "If you'd seen these roads before they were made, you'd lift up your hands and bless General Wade" give some idea of their dreadful condition before the English general and his men constructed the roads which still form the basis of some of our highland highways. On a dull day in the summer of 1934 near the 1506' summit of Drumochter, Alexander's Leyland Lion WG 2361 hurries through the Pass on the limited stop service from Inverness to Glasgow which cut right across Perthshire using the A9 from Dalnaspidal to Dunblane. Numbered P157 in the fleet, this was one of the earliest of the famous "Bluebirds" with Alexander's own coachwork which set new standards in coach travel at the time. It was operating the 10.00 a.m. departure from the Highland capital and was due in Glasgow at 6.15 p.m. which allowed a 40 minute refreshment break in Pitlochry and a further five minutes in Perth. Today's quickest Citylink journeys take only 3 ? hours over an admittedly much improved A9 road but with considerably more traffic to contend with.

The small market town of Milnathort formerly in Kinross-shire now lies within the boundaries of Perth and Kinross. In this late 1930s scene, an impatient motor cyclist overtakes Alexander's bus as it approaches the town centre. AFG 676 was a Leyland Tiger TS7 which had been new in 1935, numbered P213 in the fleet and one of fifteen similar vehicles acquired in 1937 when the company absorbed the associated General Motor Carrying Co., of Kirkcaldy, explaining the Fife registration. Painted in the famous Bluebird livery and with Alexander's own coachwork, it was working the lengthy service from Glasgow to St. Andrews which in those pre-war days took a marathon four hours for the journey. The route was via Stirling, the Hillfoots, Tillicoultry, Yetts O' Muckhart and Kinross to Milnathort where there was a five minute halt before resuming through Fife via Strathmiglo, Auchtermuchty and Cupar to the university town. This 32 seater coach, along with its stablemates, had only a relatively short life as a single decker and was rebuilt by Alexander as a double decker to assist the efforts for greater seating capacity to help cope with wartime difficulties. Accordingly in 1943 P213 was re-numbered as R400 when it appeared in its new guise as a 53 seater with Titan TD4 specification, surviving in this form until 1960. Today, this scene remains almost the same, apart from the Commercial Hotel, to the right of the Town Hall, having been re-named The Jolly Beggars and the old-style R.A.C. roadsign has gone. This directed motorists on the main A91 road not only to Dollar and to St. Andrews but to the hamlet of Meikle Seggie on an unclassified route. Today's bus of course would be a Stagecoach and not a Bluebird.

A scene from shortly after the Second War showing Alexander's local service bus from Struan to Pitlochry, with onward connections to Perth, about to join the main A9 road at Calvine, which has been a quiet backwater since the dual carriageway bypassed the village. The contemporary road sign balances this view nicely, surmounted by the Perthshire roundel and pointing to nearby Struan Station and to Kinloch Rannoch, 13 miles distant by the B847, while Blair Atholl is 4 miles towards Pitlochry on the A9. The Ministry of Transport was established in 1919 and empowered to classify highways, which was largely done by 1922/3 with principal roads allocated A numbers and class 2 roads B numbers. The bus in this scene is WG 8144 (P565), a Leyland Tiger TS8 which had been new in 1939 and after several years of service throughout the tough wartime years was looking just a shade tired, with its rear half-drop window out of alignment and a slight sag in the roof. However, the Alexander bodywork was to receive a full overhaul and repaint to Bluebird colours around 1947, when the livery was reversed, with cream predominating instead of blue. The route to Struan had been originally operated by the Pitlochry Motor Co. Ltd., an independent firm started by Marcus Russell in the early 1920s and which sold out to Alexander in 1929 although it continued to run under the P.M.C. name until merging totally in 1942. In 1971 the Struan service passed to Elizabeth Yule of Pitlochry.

The scenes on this page and the next date from 1950 in Pitlochry. Alexander's P567 (WG 8146) was a Leyland Tiger TS8 of 1939 which spent most of its life at Pitlochry depot and was a stablemate of P565 on p.49. It is seen here setting out for Dunkeld and Perth and weaving its way between parked vehicles at the lower end of the main street which is now by-passed by the A9 but nevertheless can still become congested with tourist traffic during the summer season. The Py plate which signified Alexander's code for Pitlochry may be seen below the fleet number and the twelve vehicle depot enjoyed autonomy for many years until it was reduced in status, becoming a sub-depot of Perth.

Another "Bluebird" based at Pitlochry for much of its service was PA66 (BMS 693), an Alexander bodied Leyland Tiger PS1 of 1948 and of particular interest since it was the first member of the fleet to be converted for one man operation. It replaced a wartime utility Bedford OWB in 1959 on the rural route between Pitlochry and Kinloch Rannoch where it was stabled overnight, working back on the 7.30 a.m. run each weekday morning. This scene, however, shows it bound for Perth at the bus stop in Main Street adjacent to the Butter Memorial fountain which had stood at this location since 1887 until its removal in the mid 1960s. Additional wheels in this view are provided by a timber-laden Seddon lorry and a typical post-war period pram.

Blethering at Blairgowrie. Today's computerised bus scheduling systems seldom make allowance for any more than minimum turn-around time at terminal points. Thus it is now rare to see a leisurely scene such as this from less stressful times in the early 1950s with the crews enjoying a few minutes to catch up with gossip. Alexander's Blairgowrie depot in Haugh Road, Rattray had been inherited from S.M.T. in 1949 along with routes which had formerly been part of the Scottish Motor Traction Dundee area services, including that from Blair to Perth via Coupar Angus, Burrelton, Kinrossie and Balbeggie. The buses seen here also originated with S.M.T. and had been based at their former depot in the appropriately named Terminus Street, Blairgowrie before the move to Rattray in 1946. They were P845 (CSF 253) of 1939, a Leyland Tiger TS8 and P838 (ASF 389) a 1937 Tiger TS7, both with Alexander bodywork and displaying the B∟ depot code plate for Blairgowrie. After withdrawal from the Alexander fleet in 1955, P838 saw service for a further few years with Tait & Park of Stromness then Spence of St. Margaret's Hope, two operators in the Orkney Islands.

The Christison family started a carriers business in the days of horse-drawn transport during the 1890s in the Broxburn area of West Lothian and commenced their first bus service between there and Bathgate in 1923 using the name "Progressive Motor Service." In 1926 James Christison moved to Blairgowrie where competition was less intensive and introduced a service to Kirriemuir via Alyth, Ruthven and Airlie using SF 3801, a red-liveried Eaton bodied Reo Speed Wagon still bearing the name Progressive of Broxburn on the rear panels. James then moved to open up another new run between Dundee and Arbroath with the same bus, leaving Colin Christison to continue the Kirriemuir service with SX 2333, a 14 seat Reo Junior. Thornycroft then Albion vehicles followed, one of which was GS 4145, this Victor model of 1934, with 20 seat coachwork built by Jackson of Dunfermline and seen outside the premises of Alexander McAra, the Albion agency in Dundee. In 1960 A&C McLennan of Spittalfield acquired Christison's service between Blairgowrie and Kirriemuir.

James Alexander Thomson Docherty started his transport business shortly after World War 2 under the name "Gleneagles Coaches" of Auchterarder but soon changed to "Midland Coaches" in 1947. This, of course, was many years prior to the same title being used by Alexander of Falkirk, who adopted the "Midland" name in 1961 for their services in central Scotland when that company was divided into three separate sections. Docherty's first bus was a pre-war Bedford 20 seater acquired in 1947 along with contracts and services between Dunning and Auchterarder and Kinkell Bridge and Auchterarder previously operated by Peter Stevens of Dunning. James Docherty junior took over the reins of the family business in 1975 after having served an engineering apprenticeship with A.& C. McLennan of Spittalfield at their Perth depot. Jim built up the private hire and touring side of the firm then on de-regulation of bus services in 1986 Midland Coaches obtained licences to operate from Perth to Dunblane, later extending through to Stirling. Docherty's business also incorporated a fleet of mainly Volvo lorries working on general haulage and contracts for road building. These were painted in a green livery as opposed to the black and white coaches. Today's immaculate "Midland Coaches" fleet is now in the hands of the third Docherty generation and includes predominantly Scania and Volvo coaches. Emphasis is now firmly on the coaching side of the business, with the lorry fleet reduced to only 3 from its maximum of 15 around 1980. Illustrated is AG 4149, one of Docherty's earliest buses, a Leyland Tiger TS1 with bodywork originally by Brush of Loughborough purchased in 1929 by Scottish Transport of Kilmarnock and later absorbed into the Western S.M.T. fleet where in 1936 it received a new body built by Burtenshaw of Reigate. It passed to Midland in 1948 via Glasgow dealers Millburn Motors and after a few years was sold for further service to James Yuille of Larkhall. It is pictured while on a private hire rounding one of the fearsome bends of the old Devil's Elbow in 1949 by which time it carried its third body, fitted in 1948 by Irvine of Salsburgh.

TGD 370, an Austin J2 six seater minibus of 1957 owned by the Scottish Co-operative Wholesale Society pauses at Fortingall Post Office on the Glen Lyon mail service which had been started over four decades earlier by David Fraser of Aberfeldy.

No publication on transport in Perthshire could possibly omit the spectacular spiral to success enjoyed by Stagecoach, the locally-based company with Brian Souter in the driving seat. The Stagecoach story has been well-documented and it is well-known that the company now has a rnge of road, rail and tramway interests both in the UK and North America. However, Perthshire firmly remains its base, with company headquarters in the Fair City where Brian's bus driver dad was employed at Alexander's Riggs Road depot for many years. De-regulation of coach services in 1980 gave the embryo Stagecoach business a kick-start when a long distance express service between Dundee, Perth and London was introduced and found favour immediately. In 1985 the bus operations of A. & C. McLennan of Spittalfield were purchased, giving Stagecoach the basis of what was later to become a much wider network of services in the county. Depicted above is FES 831W of 1981, a Duple-bodied Volvo B58 model which was the company's first brand new vehicle and ran initially on the Anglo-Scottish express route to and from London. It was later converted to a service bus to lead a less stressful life in rural Perthshire, where it is seen in Stanley on the former McLennan run from Spittalfield to Perth, with the author's son Christopher checking the timetable. Naturally a degree of sentiment surrounds this bus and accordingly it has been preserved as a tribute to its pioneering work during the formative years of Stagecoach. Today the company is very much a transport force to be reckoned with and in 2010 will celebrate 30 successful years.